最遊記

SAIYUKI

5

KAZUYA MINEKURA

SAIYUKI Vol. 5

Created by Kazuya Minekura

Translation - Alethea Nibley & Athena Nibley
Associate Editor - Lianne Sentar
Retouch and Lettering - Eva Han
Production Artist - James Dashiell
Cover Layout - Anna Kernbaum

Editor - Jake Forbes
Digital Imaging Manager - Chris Buford
Pre-Press Manager - Antonio DePietro
Production Managers - Jennifer Miller and Mutsumi Miyazaki
Art Director - Matt Alford
Managing Editor - Jill Freshney
VP of Production - Ron Klamert
President and C.O.O. - John Parker
Publisher and C.E.O. - Stuart Levy

A  Manga

TOKYOPOP Inc.
5900 Wilshire Blvd. Suite 2000
Los Angeles, CA 90036

E-mail: info@TOKYOPOP.com
Come visit us online at www.TOKYOPOP.com

ISBN: 1-59182-655-1

First TOKYOPOP printing: November 2004

10 9 8 7 6 5 4 3 2 1

Printed in the USA

The Story So Far

After the combination of youkai magic and science caused the youkai-maddening Minus Wave, the beautiful Shangri-La lies in chaos. Three unusual youkai and a Sanzo Priest travel West to stop the revival of Gyumaoh and save their crumbling world...bu crumbling among them, too, is the razor-thin patience that barely keeps our heroes from beating each other senseless.

Unable to escape the memory of his late sister and lover, Hakkai suffered at the hands o Chin Yisou and his vengeful psychological torture. As the goal was to break rather thar kill Hakkai, Gojyo and the others were one by one targeted by Chin Yisou's sick games Hakkai ended near the breaking point, but discovering Chin Yisou's ties to his sister's rapist forced Hakkai to make a choice--was he the Cho Gonou of the past, or the Cho Hakkai of the present? Only in releasing his blood-soaked past could he overcome the villain that hailed from it.

Meanwhile, Gyokumen Koushu stepped up her plans to revive Gyumaoh. She removed Kougaiji from Sanzo-hunting duty and instead handed him a new mission: find the other Tenchi Kaigen sutras and donate them to the experimentation. Yisou's true intention...?

Genjyo Sanzo –

A very brutal, worldly priest. He drinks, smokes, gambles and even carries a gun. He's looking for the sacred scripture of his late master, Sanzo Houshi. He's egotistical, haughty and has zero sense of humor, but this handsome 23-year-old hero also has calm judgment and charisma. His favorite phrases are "Die" and "I'll kill you." His main weapons are the Maten Sutra, a handgun, and a paper fan for idiots. He's 177cm tall (approx. 5'10"), and is often noted for his drooping purple eyes.

Son Goku –

The brave, cheerful Monkey King of legend; an unholy child born from the rocks where the aura of the Earth was gathered. His brain is full of thoughts of food and games. To pay for crimes he committed when he was young, he was imprisoned in the rocks for five hundred years without aging. Because of his optimistic personality, he's become the mascot character of the group; this 18-year-old of superior health is made fun of by Gojyo, yelled at by Sanzo and watched over by Hakkai. He's 162cm tall (approx. 5'4"). His main weapon is the Nyoi-Bo, a magical cudgel that can extend into a sansekkon staff.

Sha Gojyo –

Gojyo is a lecherous kappa (water youkai). His behavior might seem vulgar and rough at first glance (and it is), but to his friends he's like a dependable older brother. He and Goku are sparring partners, he and Hakkai are best friends, and he and Sanzo are bad friends (ha ha!). Sometimes his love for the ladies gets him into trouble. Because of his unusual heritage, he doesn't need a limiter to blend in with the humans. His favorite way of fighting is to use a shakujou, a staff with a crescent-shaped blade connected by a chain; it's quite messy. He's 184cm tall (approx. 6'), has scarlet hair and eyes, and is a 22-year-old chain smoker.

Cho Hakkai –

A pleasant, rather absent-minded young man with a kind smile that suits him nicely. It's sometimes hard to tell whether he's serious or laughing to himself at his friends' expense. His darker side comes through from time to time in the form of a sharp, penetrating gaze, a symbol of a dark past. As he's Hakuryu's (the white dragon) owner, he gets to drive the Jeep. Because he uses kikou jutsu (Chi manipulation) in battle, his "weapon" is his smile (ha ha!). He's 22 years old, 181cm tall (approx. 5'11") and his eyes are deep green (his right eye is nearly blind). The cuffs he wears on his left ear are Youkai power limiters.

THREE YEARS EARLIER.

MASS MURDER...?
Half the population of a Village was killed two months ago.
And the other day, another thousand of Hyakugan Maoh's tribe.
A THOUSAND YOUKAI, HM?
That's right.
ゴポッ
Genjyo Sanzo.
We would like you...
...to apprehend this felon.
YES?

His name is Cho Gonou.
He's a young man who once was human.

第24話

CHAPTER 24:
BE THERE <1>

RELAX. I'M NOT GONNA TAKE EVERYTHING *THIS* EARLY.

THE NIGHT'S STILL YOUNG, BOYO.

ARE ALL THE CHICKS ON GOJYO'S SIDE? UNBELIEVABLE.
OF COURSE WE ARE.
...MMM, AND WHAT GORGEOUS HAIR. HOW DID YOU SAY YOU DYE IT?
AND YOUR EYES ARE WINE RED UP CLOSE.
......

...WINNING WITH A FEW STALE BETS KEEPS THE MEALS COMING.

AND LANDING CHICKS WITH LAME PICKUP LINES GETS ME THROUGH THE NIGHT.

DAMN. LIFE IS SO EASY IT MAKES ME WANNA PUKE.

I GUESS IT WORKS IF I DON'T LOOK ANYONE IN THE EYE.

GORGEOUS HAIR, SHE SAYS.

RIIIGHT.

NOT WHEN IT'S THE COLOR OF...

HM?

WHAT THE HELL?
WAY TO BLOCK THE PATH.

EWW...
THOSE'RE A LOTTA GUTS.
HEY, MAN.
YOU DEAD DOWN THERE?

TWITCH
HUNH.
GUESS THAT'S A NO.

HE LOOKED AT ME...AND SMILED, I THINK.

......
THIS ISN'T WHAT I EXPECTED.
HELL IS RATHER ANTI-CLIMACTIC.

WHO'RE YOU CALLING ANTI-CLIMACTIC?

ABOUT TIME YOU WOKE UP.

...UH, EXCUSE ME.

ズキ

*SHARP PAIN

ARE YOU THE ONE WHO HELPED ME?

WHY? ARE YOU MAD?

HUH?

THAT THIS ISN'T HELL, I MEAN.

I TAKE IT YOU *WANTED* TO DIE.

NO.

I'M... GLAD I'M STILL HERE.

THANK YOU VERY MUCH.

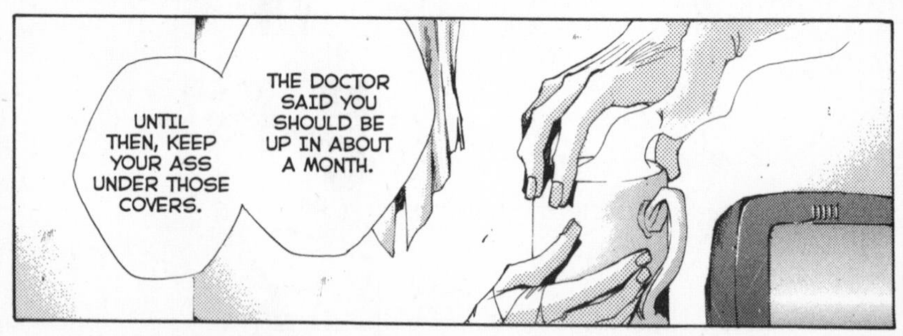

PRIEST SANZO!

THANK HEAVEN YOU'VE RETURNED!

WHAT IS IT NOW?

AS YOU CAN SEE...

FILTHY
HEY!
SANZO'S HOME. YAAAY! ♡
PANT
PANT
HE BROUGHT THAT MUDDY DOG INTO THE TEMPLE.
IT'S BEEN BREAKING RELICS, AND WE CAN'T SEEM TO CATCH IT.
......
YOU STUPID MONKEY!
DAH!
THAT HURT! WHAT'D YOU DO THAT FOR?
SHUT YOUR MOUTH! WHAT ARE YOU, IN HEAT?
NOW WASH UP AND GET CHANGED.
OW! OW! OW! OW! OW!

AND THE DOG GOES. MOVE!

OKAY ALREADY! WAY TO BE A STINKER!

...FOR THAT, YOU DIE.

THAT BOY IS A *PEST*.

WHY DID PRIEST SANZO PICK UP SUCH A DEGENERATE IN THE FIRST PLACE?

I HAVE NO IDEA.

EEP!

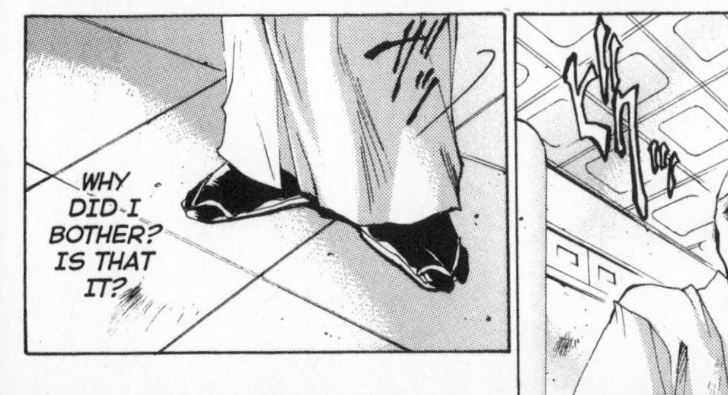

HELL IF I KNOW.
IT WAS JUST...

...HE WOULDN'T SHUT UP.

WHEN I LEFT KINZAN TEMPLE TO RECLAIM MY MASTER'S SUTRA, I DIDN'T EVEN KNOW WHERE TO START.
I'D JUST COME TO THIS TEMPLE. IT WAS THE EASTERNMOST ON THE SHORTEST ROUTE TO INFORMATION.

HIS... INCESSANTLY AGGRAVATING VOICE WOULDN'T STOP CALLING ME.
I FIGURED I'D KNOCK HIM ONE IN THE HEAD.

BUT THEN HE LOOKED UP.

WHEN HE STARED AT ME WITH THAT STUPEFIED LOOK...

SHUT THE HELL UP.
...I LOST THE URGE TO HIT HIM.
C'MON. IT'S NOT LIKE I HAVE A CHOICE.

BUT REGARDLESS, I KNOW BETTER NOW.
ONE BLOW TO THE HEAD NEVER WOULD'VE CUT IT.
SANZO!

ARE YOU GOIN' SOME-WHERE?
chink
LOOKS LIKE IT.

I JUST GOT AN IRRITATING MISSION TO GO FIND SOMEONE.
I MAY BE GONE AWHILE.
FOR REAL?

THEN LEMME COME! ♡
NEVER.
GET SOMEONE ELSE TO TAKE YOU FOR A WALK.

ARE YOU CALLIN' ME AN ANIMAL?!
SELF-AWARENESS, MONKEY. LEARN IT.

WHAT'S THE MATTER, GOKU?

SIT GAWKING LIKE THAT, AND I WILL LEAVE YOU BEHIND.

WAH! WAIT UP, WAIT UP!
SANZO, OI!

FWAP
FULL HOUSE, IT SEEMS.

HUNH. YOU'RE NOT BAD AT THIS.
THOUGH I'M GOING EASY ON ON YOU, SINCE YOU'RE INJURED.
LIKE HELL I AM.
AH. SORRY ABOUT THAT.

YOU HAVEN'T ASKED ME YET...
...ABOUT MY AFFAIRS.

FEH. YOUR BUSINESS AIN'T MINE.

I'M SORRY, BUT...
...MAY I STAY HERE UNTIL I'M WELL ENOUGH TO MOVE ON?
GOT SOME-WHERE TO GO?
NO.
THOUGH I HAVE JUST ONE THING...
...I NEED TO DO.

BUT READING THE FLOW OF THE GAME CAN ONLY GET ONE SO FAR.

NOTHING COMES WITHOUT A BIT OF *LUCK.*

JACK OF ALL TRADES AND MASTER OF NONE?

I GUESS THAT'S ME.

THEN JOIN THE CLUB.

THIS CHO GONOU KILLED LOTSA GUYS, RIGHT?
HE MUST BE PRETTY BAD.
WHO KNOWS?

WE HAVE NO CLUES BEYOND WHAT THE MAN LOOKS LIKE.
THIS ENTIRE MISSION IS MAKING ME UNEASY.
WHY WOULD THE THREE ASPECTS SEND SOMEONE OF MY STATUS AFTER AN ORDINARY MURDERER IN THE FIRST PLACE?

UNLESS THERE'S SOMETHING ELSE GOING ON HERE.
...THIS STINKS.
GOJYO'S BEEN REALLY COLD LATELY, DON'T YOU THINK?
AND HE LEFT EARLY AGAIN YESTER-DAY.
I HEARD HE PICKED UP AN INJURED GUY 'BOUT A MONTH AGO.

THE DOCTOR SAID IT WAS A DUDE...
...WITH GREEN EYES AND A PRETTY FACE.

MM?
HEY.

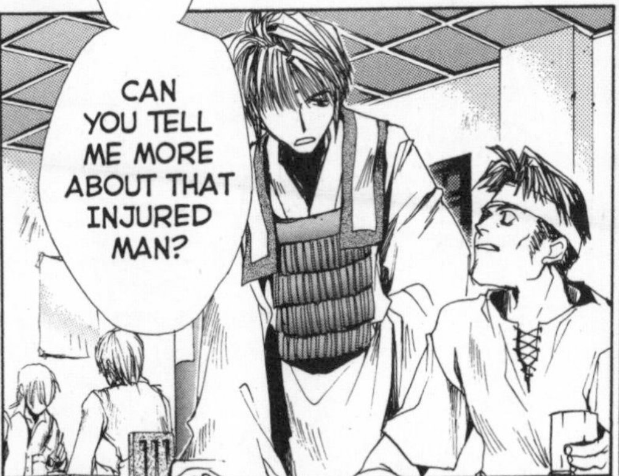
CAN YOU TELL ME MORE ABOUT THAT INJURED MAN?

WOW. LOOKIT THE BOMB-SHELL WE'VE GOT HERE.
YOU DIG MEN, PRIESTY?
I'LL TELL YOU ABOUT GREEN-EYES.

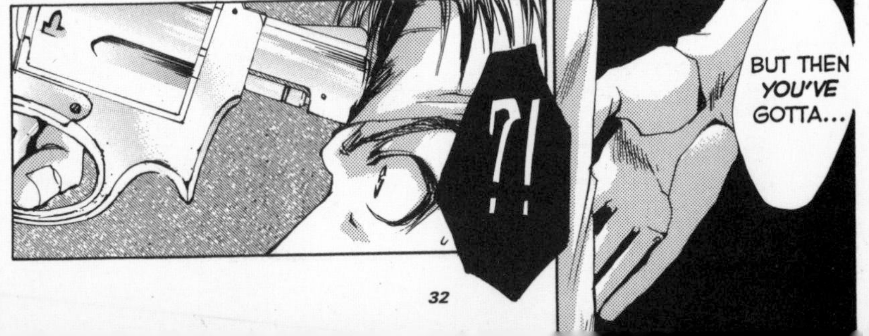
BUT THEN *YOU'VE* GOTTA...
?!

I'VE "GOTTA" WHAT?
SHIT-EATING MOTHER-FUCKER.

AH, GOJYO-SAN.
キィ

DO YOU HAVE A MOMENT?
SURE.

バサ
YOU LEAVING ALREADY?
YES.

BUT BEFORE I GO...
...I'D LIKE TO TELL YOU SOMETHING.

I'VE KILLED A LOT OF PEOPLE IN THE NAME OF REVENGE.

BUT REALLY, MORE THAN ANYTHING... I DID IT FOR MYSELF.

PERHAPS STAYING HERE SPURRED THE EPIPHANY OF MY SIN.

EPIPHANY?

I HAVE ONE LAST ACTION TO TAKE...

...AND THEN I'LL ACCEPT WHATEVER PUNISHMENT I DESERVE.

THANK YOU VERY MUCH FOR HELPING ME.

IT'S YOUR HAIR AND EYES, GOJYO-SAN.

THE RED THAT STAINED MY HANDS...
...KEPT ME GROUNDED WHEN I TRIED TO ESCAPE THE WEIGHT OF MY CRIMES.
YOUR HAIR AND EYES REMIND ME OF THAT.
THEY'RE LIKE A WARNING, I SUPPOSE.

......

'S THAT RIGHT?

I'LL BE GOING, THEN.

SURE.

HOLD THAT THOUGHT.

YEAH, YEAH.

WHO IS IT?

SORRY TO BOTHER YOU THIS LATE.

I'M LOOKING FOR SOME-ONE.

HIS NAME IS CHO GONOU.

第25話
CHAPTER 25:
BE THERE <2>

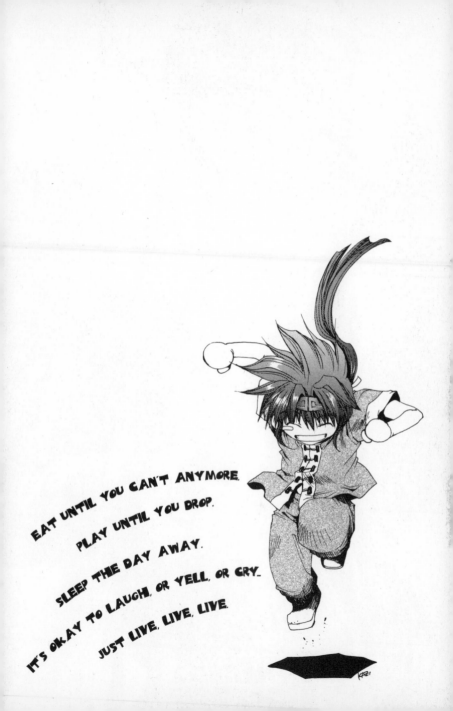

EAT UNTIL YOU CAN'T ANYMORE.
PLAY UNTIL YOU DROP.
SLEEP THE DAY AWAY.
IT'S OKAY TO LAUGH, OR YELL, OR CRY...
JUST LIVE, LIVE, LIVE.

I'M LOOKING FOR CHO GONOU.
HE'S A MASS MURDERER ON THE RUN.

SORRY, PAL. CAN'T HELP YOU THERE.
DON'T KNOW THE GUY.
VERY FUNNY.
BUT EVERYONE IN TOWN SAID YOU PICKED HIM UP, SO CUT THE BULLSHIT.
I'D SUGGEST YOU STOP HIDING HIM AND GET THE HELL OUT OF HERE.
......!!
DO YOU EVEN KNOW WHAT HE DID? HELPING HIM MAKES YOU AN ACCOMPLICE.

I SAID I'VE NEVER HEARD OF HIM.

AND WHY THE HELL'S A PRIEST LOOKING FOR A MURDERER?

......

!

!

LET GO.

YEAH? AND WHAT IF I DON'T?

!!
HGCK...
GHHK!
HAKGH!
SON OF A...
shf
!

...NOW YOU'RE DEAD, BASTARD.
HEH.
NOT EXACTLY A NORMAL PRIEST, ARE YA?

YOUR ATTI-TUDE'S GOING TO GET YOU KILLED.
NOW MOVE.
BOMBSHELL OR NOT, I DON'T ENTERTAIN GUY REQUESTS.
YOU'RE EAGER TO DIE. I CAN HELP YOU OUT WITH THAT.
GOOD LUCK TRYING.

Y-YOU'RE NOT A FRIGGIN' PRIEST!
THE NEXT ONE WILL IMPROVE THE VENTILATION IN THAT HOT HEAD OF YOURS.

GOJYO-SAN?!
!
GET YOUR ASS BACK INSIDE!
IS THAT CHO GONOU?
!!

YOU...
...BAS-TARD...
TOO BAD FOR YOU, MY GROUND HOLDS ARE KILLER. ♡

NOW HURRY UP AND GO!
I CAN'T HOLD HIM FOR-EVER.

......!

RUN, DAMMIT!

TCH!

GOKU!

YOU BROUGHT A BUDDY?
I'VE JUST GOTTA KNOCK 'IM OUT, RIGHT?
OKAY, SANZO!

......!!

NNGH...
!

—!

DAMN. HE BARELY MANAGED IT...
...BUT HE STILL BLOCKED GOKU.

HAAH...
PING
NNN.
HAA...

HEEEY, SANZO!
THIS GUY MAY BE PRETTY GOOD!
STOP SOUNDING SO HAPPY, MONKEY!

'KAY.
I'LL GET SERIOUS NOW. LOOKIE!
hop

WHA?!
WHO THE HELL IS THAT KID?!
AT THAT SPEED...
HEE HEE.
!!

THAT MAN HAS NOTHING TO DO WITH ME.

PLEASE DON'T HOLD HIM RESPON-SIBLE.

I KNOW I'VE COMMITTED VERY SERIOUS CRIMES.

AND I KNOW EVEN MY LIFE ISN'T ENOUGH FOR ATONEMENT.

BUT THERE'S ONE LAST THING...

...I STILL NEED TO DO.

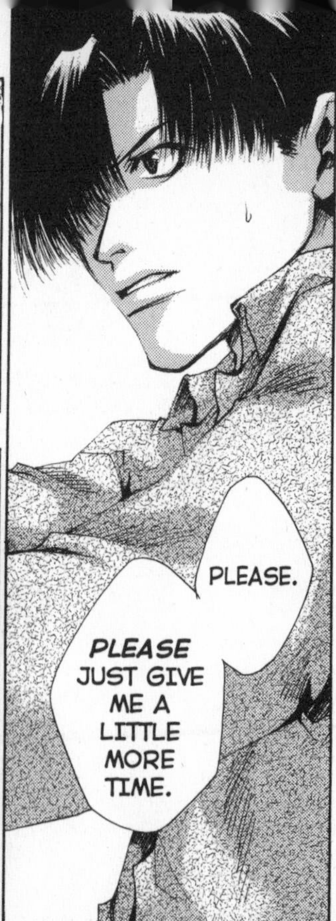
PLEASE.
PLEASE JUST GIVE ME A LITTLE MORE TIME.

I...I'M SORRY FOR DOING THIS.

WHAA?
step

H-HEY!
WAIT A SEC!
DASH

......

"I HONESTLY WAS..."
ザワ...
...HOPING TO WAKE UP IN HELL.
コポポ
I'VE FELT THAT WAY SINCE I LOST SOMEONE DEAR.
YOUR LOVER?
WELL, YES.
THAT'S HALF OF IT.
WHAT'S THAT MEAN?
ず
SHE WAS ALSO MY OLDER SISTER.
ずずず
...DO YOU THINK LESS OF ME?

AH, WHAT-EVER.
I GUESS SOME PEOPLE... GO FOR THAT.
IT WASN'T EXACTLY TALKED ABOUT.
WE WERE RAISED IN SEPARATE ORPHAN-AGES.
OUTSIDE OF THAT, WE TRIED NOT TO ADVERTISE THE FACT.
BUT STILL.
PEOPLE OFTEN HAVE A SIXTH SENSE ABOUT LOVED ONES, RIGHT?
?
WHEN SHE WAS IN DANGER...
...I DIDN'T FEEL A THING.
I WAS PLAYING WITH MY STUDENTS AT THE TIME.
WHY IS THAT, I WONDER?
WHY DIDN'T I SENSE SOMETHING AND RUN HOME?
... REALITY'S A BITCH.

YOU CAN'T BLAME ALL THAT CRAP ON YOURSELF.
IT WASN'T BECAUSE YOU DIDN'T LOVE HER ENOUGH.
AH, HELL. LIKE I'M ONE TO TALK.
I DON'T HAVE ANYTHING IMPORTANT IN MY LIFE.
I GUESS I WOULDN'T REALLY KNOW.
......
JUST ONCE, I THINK I WANNA KNOW.
WHAT EXACTLY IS LOVE?
NOT THAT I WANT IT, PARTICULARLY...
YOU DON'T NEED LOVE TO GET LAID.

I GREW OUT MY HAIR TO COVER THE SCARS FROM WHEN MY MOTHER TRIED TO KILL ME.

AS A LESSON TO MYSELF, I GUESS YOU COULD SAY. I THOUGHT I WAS THE ONLY ONE WHO SAW THAT RED AS THE WARNING COLOR OF BLOOD.

THE LOVE I COULDN'T GET, AND THE LOVE HE COULDN'T PROTECT.

...WE'RE WATCHING ILLUSIONS FADE INTO A SEA OF BLOOD.

WHILE BLAMING OUR OWN POWERLESSNESS...

SO. CHO GONOU, HUH?

THE NAME DOESN'T FIT HIM.

YOU REALLY DIDN'T ASK HIM ANYTHING?

THAT'S WHAT I'VE BEEN SAYING ALL ALONG.

ANY-WAY...

うはっ
HEEEY! THIS IS YUMMY!
CAN I EAT IT ALL?
WHY DO I HAVE TO FEED YOUR DAMN PET?!

YOU PLANNIN' TO CLEAN ME OUT, MONKEY?
DROP THE GOODS!
ぎゃあ
I'M NOT A MONKEY, I'M SON GOKU! NYAA!
GIMME GIMME!
SHUT IT! STUPID MONKEY FITS YOU BETTER.
ぎゃあ

APPARENTLY GOKU HASN'T EATEN IN 500 YEARS.
HIS BODY'S MAKING UP FOR LOST TIME.
WHA?
WHAT'D YOU SAY?
I HOPE YOU'RE KIDDING.

BUT YOU STILL MAKE ME WONDER.
WHY HIDE GONOU AND GET IN TROUBLE FOR IT?

WHY?
BEATS THE HELL OUTTA ME.

HEY, SANZO. IS GONOU A BAD GUY?
WHAT WAS THAT?
I DUNNO, IT'S WEIRD.
HE DIDN'T SEEM REAL BAD TO ME.

WHETHER THIS WORLD IS EVIL OR NOT...

...THE ONES WITH THE STRONGEST WILL TO LIVE ARE THE ONES WHO SURVIVE.

THE WILL TO LIVE.

HUNH...

HA HA
WHAT A SHAME YOU BECAME A MONK.
WHAT'S *THAT* SUPPOSED TO MEAN?
HANDS OFF.

YEAH?

BUT HE GOT AWAY, SANZO. IZZAT OKAY?

NO. THIS IS A MISSION, AS MUCH AS IT PAINS ME TO SAY SO.

WE'LL HAVE TO GO AFTER HIM.

BAH. I THINK YOU'RE WASTING YOUR TIME.

WHICH IS ALL THE MORE REASON TO GO AFTER HIM.

I'VE BEEN ORDERED TO BRING CHO GONOU TO SHAYOU PALACE.
THIS MISSION IS BAD ENOUGH WITHOUT HIM *DYING* ON ME.

LET'S GO, GOKU.
SORRY FOR THE TROUBLE.
HANG ON A SEC.

I WANNA GO TOO.

IF LETTING HIM DIE IS THE KIND THING TO DO...
...THEN I...

...MUST BE ONE SELFISH BASTARD.

Huff

Huff

ずる...

OW.

HAH HAH

I MUST HAVE REOPENED THAT WOUND.

I'M NOT SURPRISED.

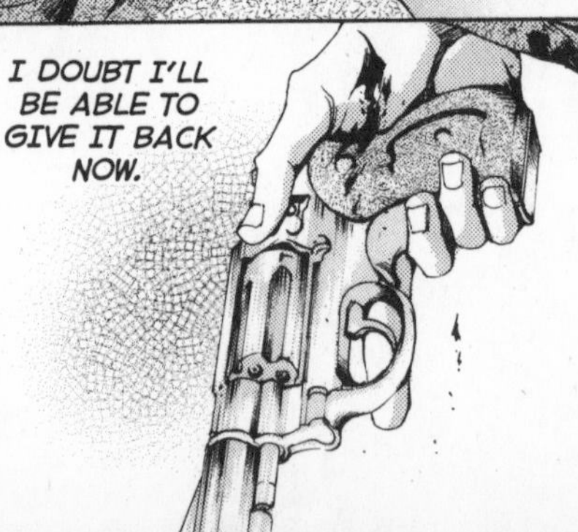

ジャラ…

......

KANAN.
NOT MUCH LONGER NOW.

WITH YOUR REMAINS, I AT LEAST WANT TO...
...WITH THESE TWO HANDS, I STILL WANT TO...

......
?!!
HGCK!

THERE YOU ARE, CHO GONOU.
IT'S ABOUT DAMN TIME.
GGG!
DO YOU REMEMBER THE FACES OF MY FAMILY?

OR THE FACES OF ALL THOSE VILLAGERS?
TELL ME YOU REMEMBER SOMETHING OF YOUR VICTIMS, MURDERER!
...HUH?

第26話
CHAPTER 26:
BE THERE <3>

I CAN'T BELIEVE I FINALLY FOUND YOU.
HERE.
I WANTED TO GIVE YOU THIS.
......!!
TOSS

SOME-
THING
WRONG?

UH,
NO.
I'M
JUST...
HEARING
THINGS. I
THINK.
I CAN
GUESS
WHERE
HE'S
HEADED.
PROBABLY
TOWARD...
...HYAKUGAN
MAOH'S
CASTLE--

HEY,
PRIEST.
WHAT'S
GONNA
HAPPEN
TO HIM IF
YOU CATCH
HIM?

YOU'RE IN DANGER OF SOUNDING ATTACHED.

AFTER I SAVED HIS DAMN LIFE?

A STUPID DEATH WOULD PISS ME OFF.

OI.

PAT

YOU'RE A PRETTY HIGH PRIEST, YEAH? THEN YOU PROBABLY KNOW.

WHAT DO RED HAIR AND EYES MEAN?

THE COLOR OF *BLOOD.*

HE THINKS THIS RED IS FOR *PENANCE.*

SO DO I.

AN UNBREAKABLE CURSE.

CALL ME GREEDY IF YOU HAVE TO...

...BUT I WANT THE GUY TO LIVE.

......

*SHAVING THE HEAD IS ASSOCIATED WITH BECOMING A BUDDHIST MONK.

WHAT THE HELL WAS *THAT*, CHIMPY?!
WHAT IS IT WITH YOU TWO MAKING ME BALD?!
BLAH. IT'S AS COLD AS THE REST OF YA.
HUH?
I THOUGHT IT MIGHT BE HOT.
IT'S AS BRIGHT AS SOMETHIN' BURNIN'.
YOU'RE AS STUPID AS YOU LOOK.

EXACTLY WHAT ARE YOU EXPECT-ING?

I-I GREW MY HAIR OUT.

I TRIED TO SAVE SOMEONE WHO THOUGHT I WAS IMPORTANT.

BUT THE ONE WHO WANTS TO BE SAVED...

...IS ME.

WHAT IS IT?
I'M SMELLIN' BLOOD.

?!
WHICH WAY?

RIGHT. MOVE!

UM...

OVER THERE!

FROM WHEN YOU TOOK MY BROTHER...

...AND RIPPED HIS *EYES* OUT.

THE SACRIFICE OF YOUR SINGLE LOVER SAVED ALL THOSE HUMANS.

BUT YOU...

...DESTROYED EVERYTHING THAT SACRIFICE WAS FOR!

BE MY GUEST.
IT'S NOT AS IF I NEED THEM.
?!!
HEY!

ALL RIGHT.
LET ME GET YOU THE OTHER ONE.

I UNDERSTAND HOW YOU FEEL.
おっ
S-SON OF A...
グッ
CUT...

...THAT
...
...OUT!
ARGH!
WHAT
THE--
OW!
OW
OW
OW!
WHAT'RE
YOU
DOIN',
STUPID?!
HUH?
THAT'S
NOT
COOL!
I THINK
YOUR
EYES ARE
REALLY
PRETTY!
CRUNCH

WAS IT YOU WHO SAID RED IMPLIES REPENTANCE?

...BUT DYING ALONE WON'T CHANGE A THING.

TRUST ME ON THAT ONE.

WE KNOW YOU WANNA KILL HIM.
GO AHEAD-- WE WON'T STOP YOU.
JUST REMEMBER...
PEOPLE WHO KILL CAN'T EXPECT TO BE SPARED.
KARMA SEES TO THAT.

OR SO SAYS SOME WORLDLY MONK.
WHATEVER *THAT'S* WORTH.

NNGH!

J-JUST DIE, YOU SICKO!

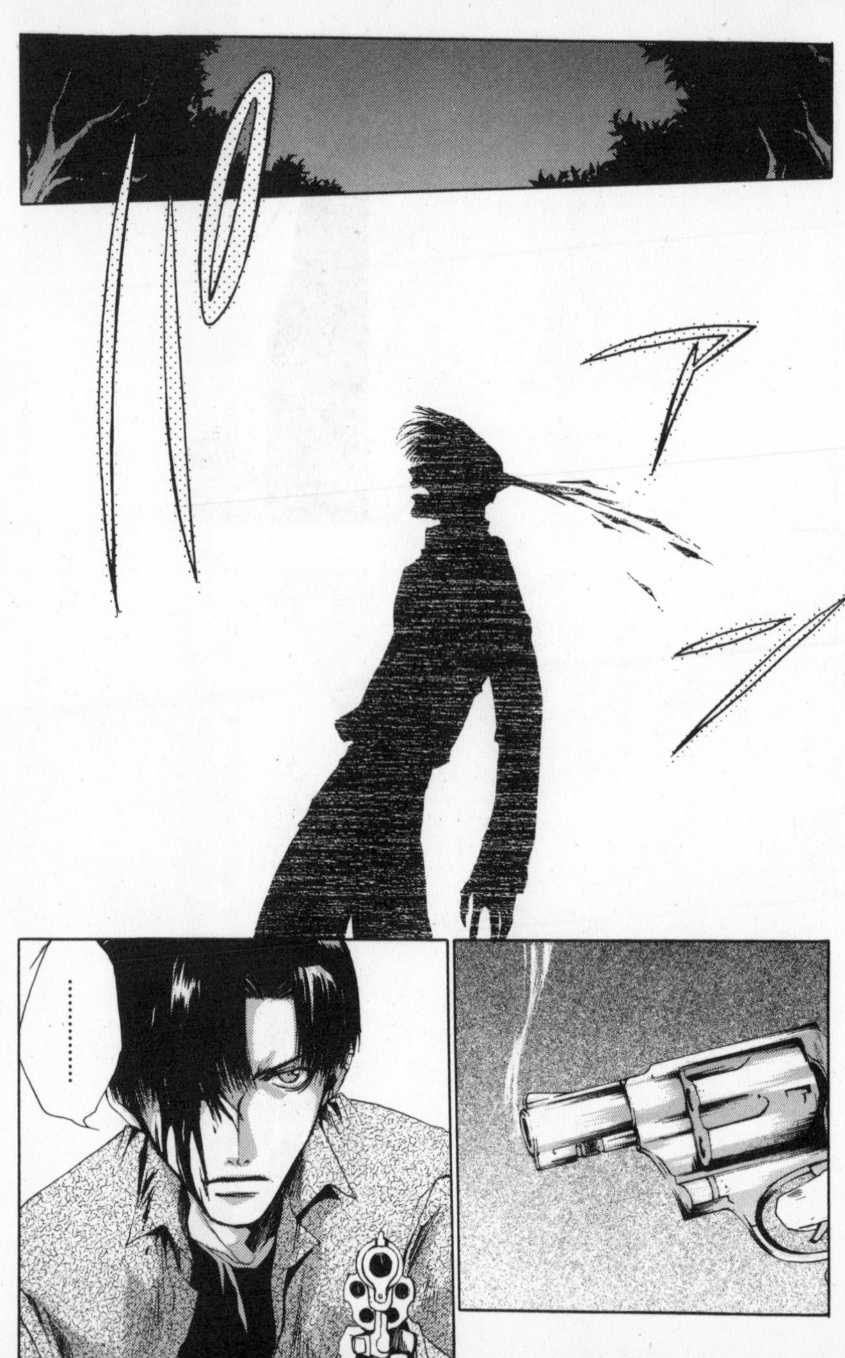

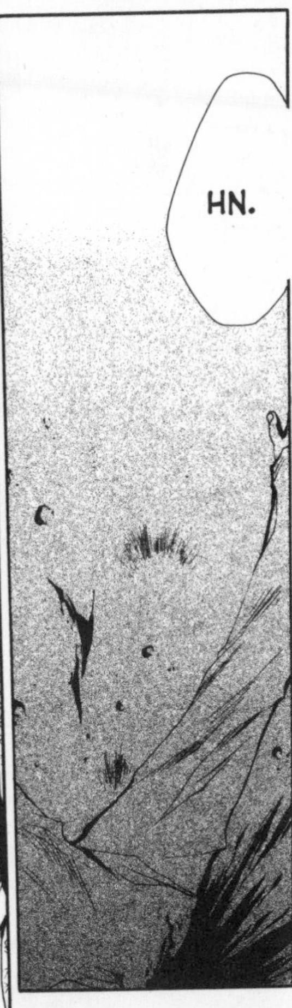

IT DOESN'T MATTER WHERE I LOOK.

IT'S ALWAYS *IDIOTS* AS FAR AS THE EYE CAN SEE.

CAN YOU WALK?

UM, YES.

CHO GONOU.

I HOPE YOU LIKE COMPANY.

HUH?

WHAT... HAPPENED...?
A FIRE, IT LOOKS LIKE.
SOMEONE PROBABLY BURNED THE CASTLE DOWN A FEW DAYS AGO.

NOT MUCH LEFT, IS THERE?

...SO THAT'S IT, THEN.

AGAIN.
I COULDN'T SAVE HER *AGAIN.*

DUDE. READ A *SUTRA* OR SOME-THING.
C'MON, MR. WORLDLY PRIEST.
HUNH.

I DON'T THINK IT WOULD HELP MUCH.

C'MON, MAN.
IS THAT A REASON NOT TO?

......

crunch

FINE. BUT WHEN I READ A SUTRA...
...IT'S NOT FOR THE DEAD.

IT'S LIKE ALL THE CONFLICT IN US HAS VANISHED.

I DIDN'T KNOW HIS VOICE COULD GET SO CLEAR.

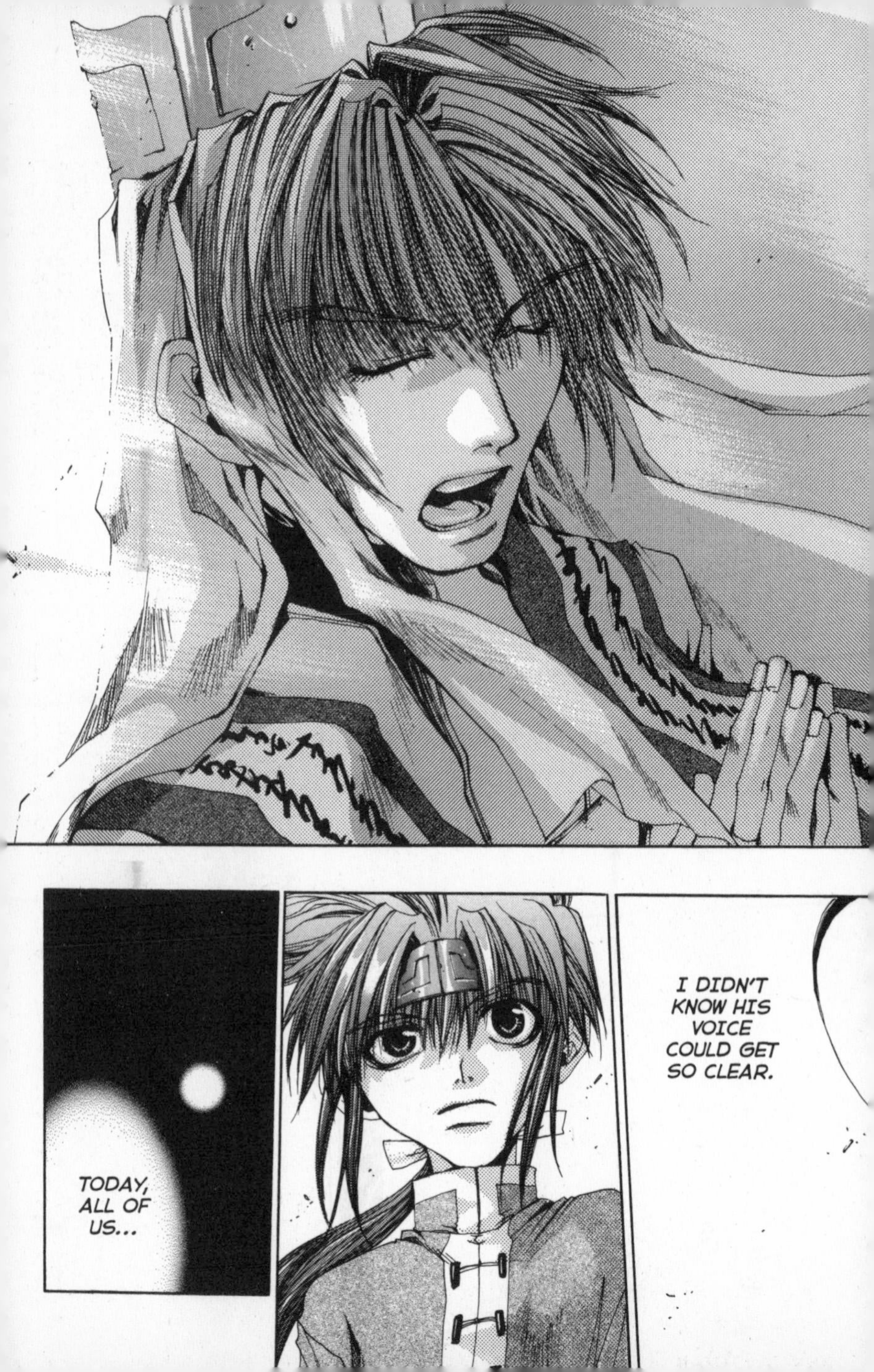

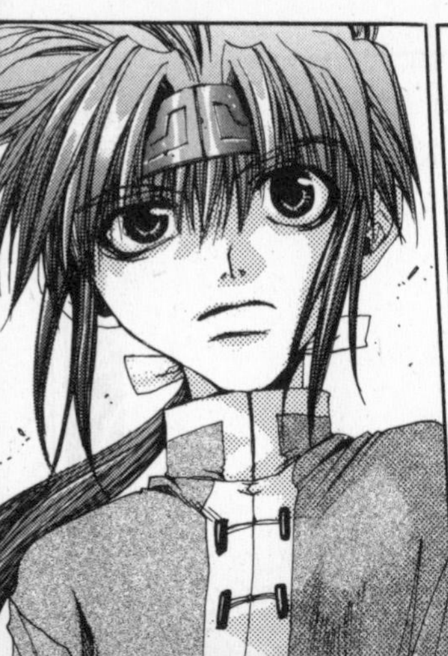

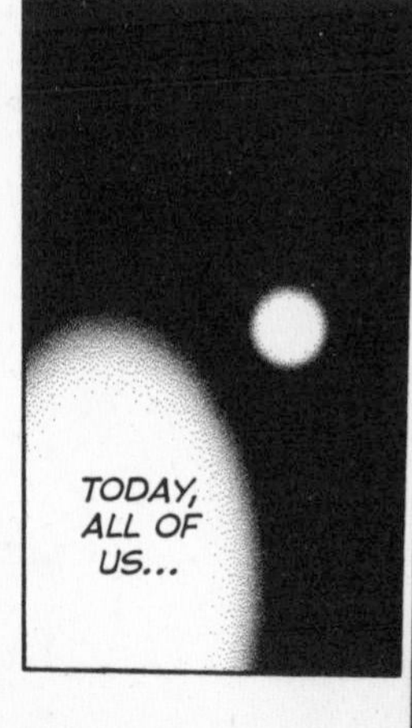
TODAY, ALL OF US...

...HAVE BEEN BROUGHT TOGETHER UNDER THIS GOLDEN LIGHT.

オォ

オ

THERE'S NO NEED FOR THAT.

BUT...
I DON'T MIND, REALLY.
PLEASE CONTINUE.

CLANK
......

Priest Genjyo Sanzo, criminal Cho Gonou.
Enter and come forth.

"IT'S AS BRIGHT AS SOMETHIN' BURNIN'. I THOUGHT IT MIGHT BE HOT."

EVERYWHERE I GO, PEOPLE SAY WHATEVER THE HELL THEY WANT.

"BUT DO YOU SERIOUSLY THINK BLOOD IS THE ONLY THING THAT'S RED IN THIS WORLD?

YEAH, YEAH. I KNOW.

"THEY'RE LIKE A WARNING, I SUPPOSE."

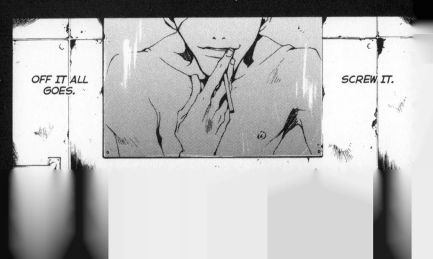

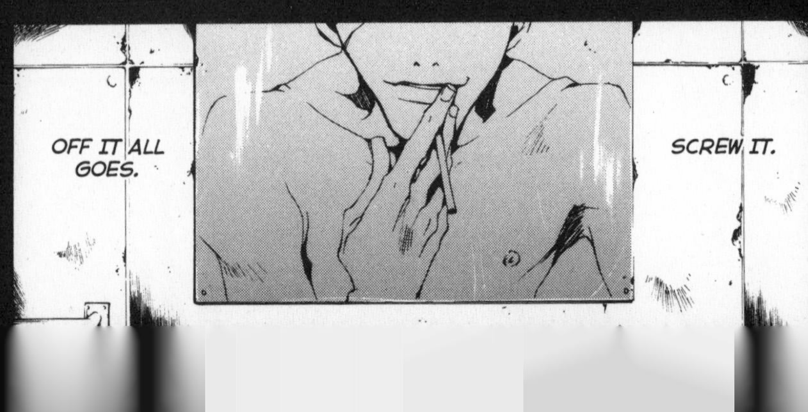

SCREW IT.
OFF IT ALL GOES.

第27話
CHAPTER 27:
BE
THERE
<4>

"CHO GONOU IS DEAD."

YOU'RE FREAKIN' *KIDDING* ME!

YOU'RE THE ONE WHO TOLD HIM TO KEEP LIVING!

STUPID BASTARD!

I TOLD YOU.

THE GODS DON'T SAVE ANYONE.

NO ONE CAN INTERFERE WITH THE FATE HE CHOSE.
NOT YOU, AND NOT ME.
flop
SON OF A... BITCH.
THIS IS THE SECOND TIME A HOTTIE'S DUMPED ME.
WERE YOU FLATTERING YOURSELF?
....
I GUESS I WAS.

GOJYO ?!
OMIGOD, IT REALLY *IS* YOU!
YO. LONG TIME.
WHAT HAPPENED TO YOUR HAIR?!
OH.
JUST... STUFF.
WE HAVEN'T SEEN YOU PLAY CARDS IN FOREVER, MEANIE.
NAH, I STILL PLAY.
I CAN'T EAT IF I DON'T WIN SOME HANDS.

THAT OLD ROUTINE!

IS THERE SOME OTHER WOMAN, GOJYO?!

I WISH.

THOUGH I DID GET CLOSE TO THIS GORGEOUS BLOND WHO WAS A REAL BITCH...

...AND THIS OTHER TART WHO'S A BIT LACKING IN THE BRAINS DEPARTMENT.

AND THAT'S NOT COUNTING THE TRAGIC AND EMOTIONALLY SCREWED BEAUTY.

HUH?
WHAT ARE YOU SAYING?
SEE YA LATER.
HEY, WAIT! GOJYO!
OOOOH!

RIGHT.
IT'S NOT LIKE ANYTHING'S CHANGED.

WHEN MY HAIR GROWS BACK, IT'LL STILL BE RED.
AND MY RED EYES'LL ALWAYS STARE BACK FROM THE MIRROR.

BUT...I'M STARTING TO THINK THAT'S OKAY.
MISS? ONE OF THESE.
YES, SIR.

THESE ARE SUCH A BEAUTIFUL RED, AREN'T THEY?

GOJYO.

...GUESS YOU COULD SAY THAT.
HEY, MISSY.
ON SECOND THOUGHT, I'LL TAKE *FOUR.*

WOOOOW! YOU GUYS!

I HAVEN'T SEEN YA IN FOREVER!

SORRY FOR THE INTRU-SION.

SHUT IT, MONKEY.

GAH!

GOJYO'S HAIR'S ALL STUPID! HA HA!

OI.

YOU TRICKED ME, YOU CHEATING PRIEST!

WHAT ARE YOU TALKING ABOUT?

BUDDHISM FORBIDS KILLING.
CRIMINAL OR NO, WE CAN'T *EXECUTE* ANYONE.
YOU HAVE A BRAIN. USE IT.
I'M GONNA DANCE ON YOUR FREAKIN' GRAVE.
COOL!
YOU'RE FREE NOW, YAH?
I AM.

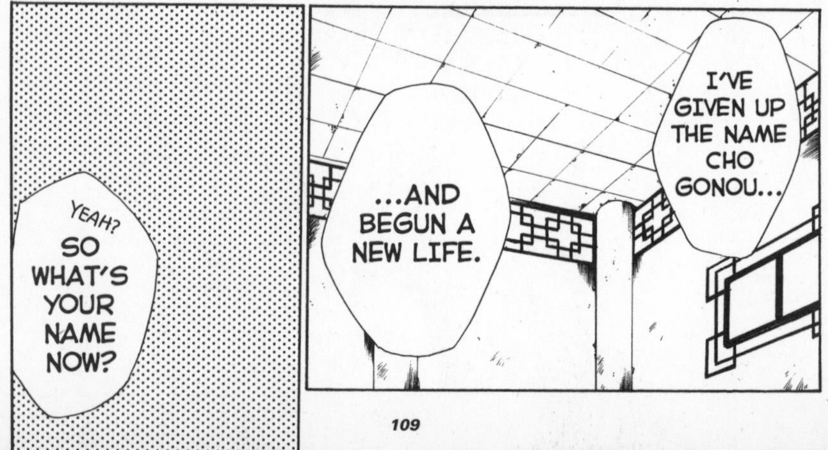

HAKKAI.

YOU LIKE IT?

...HAK-KAI.

MM! IT'S BETTER'N YOUR LAST NAME.

YOU THINK SO?

LET'S SEE HOW LONG YOUR ITTY BITTY BRAIN CAN REMEMBER THAT.

DON'T MAKE FUN OF ME! I CAN REMEMBER!

HAKKAI HAKKAI HAKKAI HAKKAI HAKKAI HAKKAI!

HOW'S THE ARTIFICIAL EYE DOING?

VERY WELL, THANK YOU.

AND I, AH...

...CONVINCED GOJYO TO LET ME STAY WITH HIM.

I'M STARTING TO THINK HE'S SUB-MONKEY.

HE NEEDS HELP REMEMBERING GARBAGE DAY.

IT'S A REASON FOR CONCERN.

NAH, HAKKAI!
HUH?
I WON'T FORGET YOUR NEW NAME!
SO DON'T CHANGE IT ANYMORE, 'KAY?
....
WE HAVE A DEAL.

WELCOME TO LIFE.

EVERYTHING'S A USELESS STRUGGLE UNTIL YOU DIE.

......
WHAT IS IT NOW?
WELL? DO YOU LIKE THE CUT?
BETTER THAN YOUR PATHETIC ANGST.

HEH HEH.

THEN GROW IT BACK OUT IT IS. ♪
I'M A PERV, SO IT GROWS FAST.
ARE YOU LOOKING FOR A FIGHT?
HOO
HOO.
HOO.

ALL RIGHTEE!
!
I'M STARVING, SO LET'S GO LAND SOME FOOD.
WHEE!
ALL RIGHT!
YIPEE! YIPEE!
JUST KEEP IT DOWN.
C'MON, SANZO! CHOW TIME!
WHAT, ME?
HMPH...
ONLY IF YOU'RE BUYING.

PRIEST SANZO, WHERE ARE YOU GOING?
THERE'S STILL BUSINESS YOU HAVEN'T--
SHUT UP AND GO TO HELL.
B-BUT PRIEST SANZO!

WOW.
WHAT A BEAUTIFUL DAY.

DAMN STRAIGHT. PICNIC WEATHER.
THEN NEXT TIME WE SHOULD PACK LUNCHES, YES?
EXCUUUSE ME!
TEACHER! ARE BANANAS A GOOD SNACK ?
SILENCE. NOW.
YOU'RE ANNOYING ME ALREADY.
DEATH IS SEEMING MORE AND MORE PREFERABLE TO YOU LOT.

THEY CERTAINLY IMPLY THEY'D BREAK ALL COMMANDMENTS WITHOUT A SECOND THOUGHT.

BUT BEINGS LIKE THAT... THEY'RE SOMETIMES MORE ELOQUENT THAN ANY DOCTRINE.

I *DO* STAND BY THAT NOTION.

YOU'RE DIGGING WAY TOO DEEP.

IT'S NOTHING THAT FANCY.

THOSE GUYS JUST HAPPENED TO BE THERE.
第28話
CHAPTER 28:
SANDSTORM

TOO...
...HOT.
!

THE GRAVE IS PLEASANTLY COOL.

AH HA HA!

I'M AFRAID THEY WOULD ROT BEFORE THEY COULD ENJOY IT.

W-WE'LL SHUT UP.

DAMN.

HAKKAI, IS THIS DESERT REALLY A SHORTCUT?

THE MAP SAYS IT ISN'T AS BIG AS IT SEEMS.

THOUGH IT *DOES* INTERFERE WITH ONE'S SENSE OF DIRECTION.

WOULD YOU LIKE A SCARY STORY TO COOL YOU OFF? ♪

I KNOW PLENTY.

UH, NO.

THE LAST PERSON I WANT FREAKING ME OUT IS YOU, HAKKAI.

HUH?

CHECK IT OUT.

HEY! GUY IN TH' BLAN-KETS!
DO YA LIVE NEAR HERE?
AND DO YOU KNOW HOW MUCH FARTHER THIS DESERT EXTENDS, PLEASE?

TRAVELERS GET LOST IN THESE PARTS A LOT.

LUCKY THIS FELLA BUMPED INTO YOU.

PARDON ME FOR ASKING ...

...BUT WHY IS THERE A VILLAGE OUT HERE?

HM. RIGHT.

THIS PLACE *USED* TO BE A DECENT TOWN.

A YEAR AGO, THE DESERT SUDDENLY EXPANDED AND SWALLOWED THE VILLAGE UP.

WE'RE JUST THE ONES WHO CAN'T LEAVE.

IS THAT RIGHT?
I GUESS THAT'S ANOTHER FORM OF THE SPREADING CHAOS.
ばさ
HUH?
?
WHATSA MATTER?
THOSE ROBES YOU'RE WEARING!
DON'T TELL ME...
...ARE YOU A *SANZO* PRIEST?!
WHO WANTS TO KNOW?

I'M SORRY, BUT YOU CAN'T STAY HERE.
FIND SOME OTHER PLACE TO SLEEP!

SLAM!
WHAA?
WHY THE HELL--

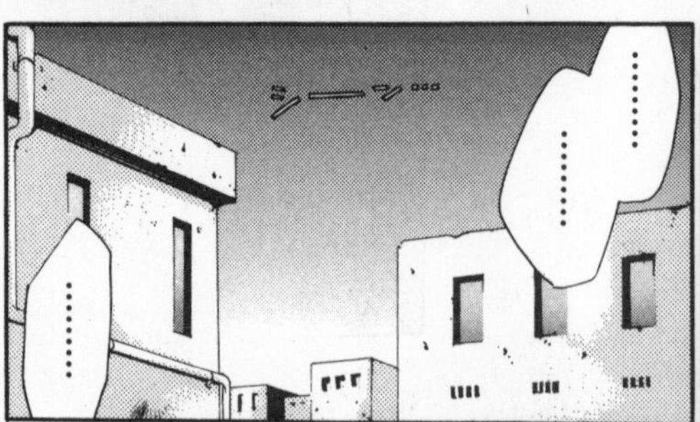
......
......
......

WHAT WAS THAT?
HOW SHOULD I KNOW?

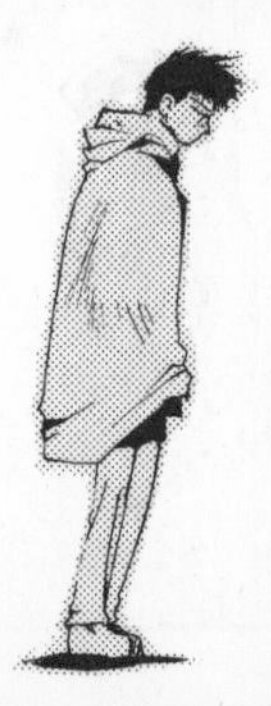
DO YOU KNOW SOMETHING OF THIS, LITTLE ONE?
WE'D APPRECIATE YOU SHARING.

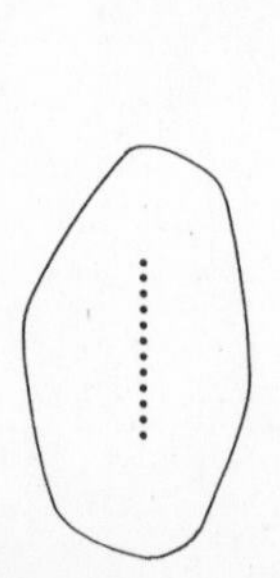
......

...ABOUT A Y-YEAR AGO.
WHEN THIS PLACE WAS STILL PART OF THE TOWN...
...A SANZO PRIEST CAME THROUGH.
HE WAS JUST RESTING FROM A TRIP--LIKE YOU GUYS.
THE WHOLE TOWN HEARD ABOUT IT AND WANTED TO COME SEE.
BUT A YOUKAI FROM THE DESERT HEARD ABOUT HIM TOO.
SHE CAME TO EAT THE SANZO PRIEST.

WOW! SHE CAME ALL TH' WAY HERE TO EAT A SANZO?
SANZOS MUST TASTE AWESOME.
I WISH IT SOUNDED LIKE YOU'RE KIDDING.
THE SPIDER WE FOUGHT SAID SOMETHING LIKE THAT.

"EATING A PRIEST WILL EXTEND YOUR LIFESPAN."

SHE SAID IT'S A SORT OF YOUKAI LEGEND.

AH. THAT WOULD MAKE A SANZO, THE HIGHEST PRIEST...

...LIKE THE BEST MEDICINE IN THE WORLD.

↑NOT QUITE RIGHT.

THEY DIDN'T STAND MUCH OF A CHANCE, SO THE SANZO ENDED UP TAKEN.

THOUGH THE YOUKAI LEFT US ALONE AFTER THAT... THE DESERT'S GOTTEN WIDER SINCE THEN.

THAT'D MAKE US BEING HERE A DANGER TO THE VILLAGERS.

MAKES SENSE. I DON'T BLAME 'EM FOR BEING DODGY.

I'M SORRY.

THE PEOPLE HERE ARE NICE, REALLY.

NAH-- YA CAN'T HELP BEIN' SCARED. 'S OKAY!

WE SHOULD PROBABLY LEAVE SOON, THEN.

......

IS SOMETHING WRONG, SANZO?
SORT OF.

DO YOU KNOW WHERE THAT DESERT YOUKAI'S BASE IS?
UM, I HAVE AN IDEA.

HEY, KID.
YES?

THEN TAKE US THERE.
HEY, WAIT A SECOND!

YOU WANNA KILL THAT THING?
SINCE WHEN ARE *WE* HEROES?
AN' SHE'S GONNA WANNA EATCHA, SANZO!
THAT THING'S PROBABLY WAY OUT OF THE WAY.

WAIT.

THAT'S YOUR "ULTERIOR MOTIVE" FACE.

....

MAYBE.

オォオォ

OUT FOR A WEE STROLL?

GODSPEED, YOUR HIGHNESS.

NOT THIS FREAKSHOW.
IF IT ISN'T NI JIANYI.
GOOD DAY TO YOU. ♡

I DON'T HAVE TIME FOR YOUR SICK HUMOR.
EXCUSE US.
THEY SAY YOU'VE BEEN TAKEN OFF THE SANZO CASE?

......
AND THIS IS ALL FOR YOUR DEAR MOTHER?
IT'S ENOUGH TO MAKE A GUY CRY.
sob
sob
APPARENTLY ONE OF THE TENCHI KAIGEN SUTRAS IS IN THE DESERT TO THE EAST.
GYOKUMEN KOUSHU MADE ME HER SUTRA FETCHBOY A WHILE AGO, NI.
SANZO'S NOT MY PROBLEM ANYMORE.
BAH.
FORGET HIM, KOU.
AH, BUT I HAVE SOMETHING I THINK YOU'D LIKE.

AREN'T YOU CURIOUS ABOUT THE GREATER TRUTH BEHIND ALL THIS?
WOULDN'T YOU LIKE TO KNOW ABOUT THE CORRUPT PARADISE THAT IS SHANGRI-LA?
I HAVE A FEW TASTY TIDBITS FOR YOU.
TAKE THE CHILDREN OF TABOO, FOR INSTANCE.
WHY IS HUMAN-YOUKAI INTERBREEDING FORBIDDEN IN THE FIRST PLACE?
EVERY LEGEND HAS A TIE TO HISTORY.
AND SCIENCE HELPS US PROVE RUMOR, OF COURSE.

CHILDREN BORN BETWEEN DIFFERENT SPECIES...
...CAN'T GENERALLY REPRODUCE, YOU KNOW.
......!!
THAT'S SOMETHING I LOOKED INTO MYSELF, BUT THERE'S PROOF.
THE CHAOS FROM MIXING YOUJUTSU AND SCIENCE...
...CAN BE ADDRESSED EVEN ON A GENETIC LEVEL.

WHO THE HELL *ARE* YOU?

WHAT ARE YOU REALLY AFTER?

I'M JUST AN ORDINARY SCIENTIST.

I WANT THE *TRUTH.*

IN THE FORM OF SOMETHING I CAN *SEE*, OF COURSE.

....
OOO...
NIIIIIIII-CHAAAAAN!

ずん
ずん
YOU TRYIN' TO GO SOMEWHERE WITHOUT LIRIN AGAIN?!
YAONE SPILLED.
FORGIVE ME, LORD.
I'M AFRAID IT SLIPPED OUT.

YOUR MOTHER SAID TO KEEP YOU IN THE CASTLE.
BE GOOD AND WAIT HERE.
BUT THAT'S A *SUCKY* PLAN!

I'LL BRING YOU BACK SOMETHING, UH, YUMMY.
HOW'S THAT?
YAAAAAAAH? ♡
HAVE A GOOD TRIP. ♥

BE SURE TO HOLD ON TO WHAT'S MOST IMPORTANT.

THE PEOPLE I LOVE...

...ARE ALREADY WHAT I LIVE FOR.

SQUEEZE

ALL THAT EXISTS IS WHAT I CAN TOUCH.

OI, SANZO.
TELL ME WHY WE'RE WASTING OUR TIME AGAIN?

THE KID SAID A SANZO PRIEST WAS TAKEN HERE.
IF HE REALLY WAS KILLED BY THAT YOUKAI...

...HIS BELONGINGS SHOULD BE IN THAT CASTLE.
INCLUDING THE TENCHI KAIGEN SUTRA EVERY SANZO CARRIES.

IT SEEMS THAT GYUMAOH'S FORCE IS GATHERING SUTRAS.
RIGHT.
WHICH IS WHY *WE* NEED TO FIND IT FIRST.
NN?

?!
WHAT THE-- NYAGH!
HEY!
M-MY BODY'S SINKIN'!
GOKU!
WHAT THE HELL'S--
!!

WHA?!
YOU'RE SHITTIN' ME!
WATCH IT, GOJYO!
DAMMIT!

!!
NNGH!
GREAT.
IS THIS A TRAP?
I'D SAY THAT'S A REASON-ABLE GUESS.
HAH!
GOKU!
GOJYO!

SNAG

JEEP ?!

ばッ
!
ッ!!
ズ
ズ
ズ...
ザ
ア...

CHEEP!

CHEEP CHEEP!

CHEEEEEP!

WHO CAN PASS JUDGMENT ON FOOLISH SHEEP?

I LAUGH TO THINK THERE'S PRIDE IN BLOODSHED.

第29話

CHAPTER 29: A FATAL DOSE

THERE YOU ARE, LADY LIRIN.
I WAS LOOKING FOR YOU.
LADY GYOKUMEN WANTS TO SEE YOU.
YO, YAONE.
YES?

I KNOW MY MAMA HATES ME.

MAYBE ONII-CHAN'S MOM'LL LOVE ME INSTEAD.

LADY LIRIN...
MAYBE SHE WON'T CARE IF I'M HER REAL KID OR NOT.
LIRIN, LISTEN.
BLOOD ISN'T EVERYTHING.
AND REMEMBER SOMETHING...
YOUR BROTHER AND I LOVE YOU VERY MUCH.

I KNOW. NYA HA!
LIRIN LOVES YOU TOO.

......
WHERE THE HELL... AM I?

I GUESS THAT YOUKAI'S LOOKING FOR COMPANY.
...AND MY ARMS WON'T MOVE. GREAT.
COME TO THINK OF IT, I CAN'T MOVE A THING.
DRUGS, MAYBE.
UREEEEE
ARE WE AWAKE ALREADY?
IT'S ALL RIGHT; THERE'S NO RUSH.
IF YOU'RE STUCK IN THAT BE,D YOU MIGHT AS WELL ENJOY IT.

I'M LIAN LI, MASTER OF THIS CASTLE.

AND HOW ARE WE FEELING, DEAR PRIEST SANZO?

LIKE... SHIT.

DAMN, EVEN MY MOUTH BARELY MOVES.

I ADMIT I'M SURPRISED.
YOU'RE THE SECOND SANZO TO WANDER TO MY HOME.

...YOU ATE THE OTHER ONE?
WITH RELISH.
HE TASTED BETTER THAN HE LOOKED.

YOU DON'T SEEM AFRAID. WHY?
N-NO REASON.
THE OTHER SANZO CHANTED A SUTRA AND ALMOST WET HIMSELF.
I THOUGHT ALL HIGH PRIESTS WERE STRAIGHT-LACED OLD MEN.
A PRETTY YOUNG THING LIKE YOU'S A TREAT.

I THINK I LIKE YOU.

SO YOU'RE ALREADY... IMMORTAL.
WHY BOTHER EATING ME?

AFTER YOU CAME ALL THE WAY HERE? NOT EATING YOU WOULD BE RUDE.
T-TELL ME.
WHAT'S THE DRAW OF BEING AGELESS?

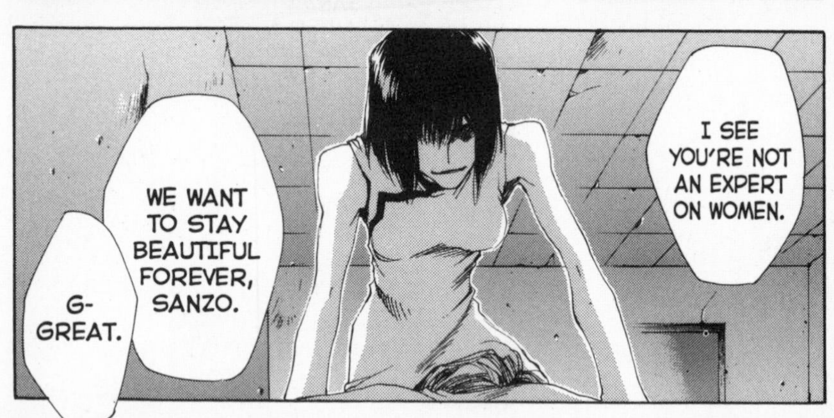
I SEE YOU'RE NOT AN EXPERT ON WOMEN.
WE WANT TO STAY BEAUTIFUL FOREVER, SANZO.
G-GREAT.

EXCUSE ME?

YOUR MAKEUP'S PRETTY... THICK.

BUT NOT THICK ENOUGH.

YOU'RE ABSOLUTELY VOMIT-WORTHY.

BUT YOU'RE NOT FOOLING ANYONE, FAGGOT.

TAKE THAT BACK, PRIEST.

YOU'RE IN NO POSITION TO THROW AROUND INSULTS.

I CAN KILL YOU WHENEVER I WANT!

YOU'RE STUCK IN THAT UGLY BODY FOR ETERNITY.

I'M NOT THE LOSER HERE.

JUST G-GET GOING.

ガッシャ
ARE YA LISTENIN', UGLIES?! OI!
ガッシャ
GIVE IT A REST, GOKU.
I DON'T THINK ASKING IS ENOUGH TO GET US OUT.

I'M SO HUUUNGRY.
I TOLD YOU TO QUIT IT.
HM. BEFORE SANZO CAN BE EATEN...
YOU USED ALL YOUR ENERGY THRASHING AT THE BARS.
...OUR GOKU JUST MAY STARVE.

.....?
TWITCH

FWAP

WHAT'S THAT SOUND?
GREAT.
YOU'RE HEARING THINGS NOW?
SOME SORTA "FWAPPY FWAPPY" SOUND LIKE--
AM NOT! IT'S LIKE... PAPER MOVIN'.

NYAAAA!

GOKU?

A SCORPION! GET IT OFF GET IT OFF!

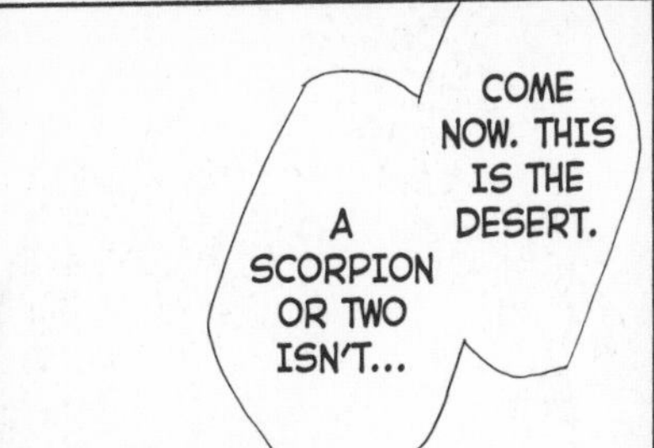

R-RIGHT. ONE OR TWO I CAN SEE.
BUT WHAT'S A MILLION SUPPOSED TO MEAN?

I DON'T THINK IT'S POSSIBLE, MASTER.

THANK YOU FOR THE THOUGHT...
...BUT I'M NOT WORTHY TO BE A SANZO PRIEST.
LISTEN TO ME, KOURYUU.
THERE WERE NEVER ANY CRITERIA FOR BECOMING A SANZO.

IT'S BEEN THIRTEEN YEARS, BUT I THINK I SEE NOW.
A SANZO NEEDS A STRONG BODY...
...BUT, MORE IMPORTANTLY, HE NEEDS A STRONG

IT'S TIME FOR YOU TO BE STRONG...
...PRIEST GENJYO SANZO.
AND THOSE WORDS OF HIS WERE THE LAST HE EVER SAID.
IT WAS THE LAST SMILE HE EVER MADE.
MY PRIESTHOOD WAS MY MASTER'S FINAL WISH.

KOUMYOU SANZO.
MY TEACHER. MY FATHER.

HE WAS THE ONLY SANZO PRIEST I EVER ACKNOWLEDGED.

THE FACT THAT I NOW CARRY MY MASTER'S NAME...

...SERVES TO REMIND ME OF MY OWN FALLIBILITY.

SPLAT

HUNH.

YOU'RE A COCKY LITTLE BASTARD, AREN'T YOU?

NNGH.

HAH.

YOU'RE ALL THE SAME IN THE END.

THERE'S NO POWER IN STUPID HUMANS READING SUTRAS!

WHAT'S SO GREAT ABOUT A SANZO PRIEST?!

...MAYBE YOU'RE RIGHT.

HGCK!
WH-
WHAT?
BUT YOU SHOULDN'T BE ABLE TO MOVE!

YOU'RE RIGHT, BY THE WAY. A SANZO'S NOTHING BUT A HUMAN.
YOUR BITCH SLAPS WERE ENOUGH TO WEAR THE DRUGS DOWN.
BUT HUMANS ARE GOOD AT KILLING.

HA HA HA!

FORGETTING SOMETHING?

GIVE ME A BREAK.

I'M *IMMORTAL*, SANZO. YOU CAN'T KILL ME!

YOU ACTUALLY BELIEVE THAT STUPID RUMOR?

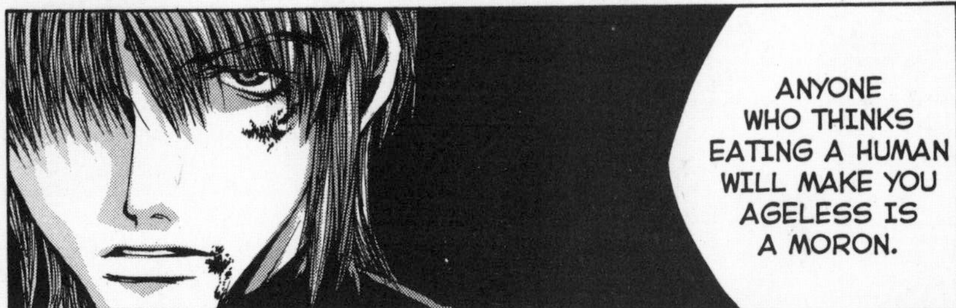

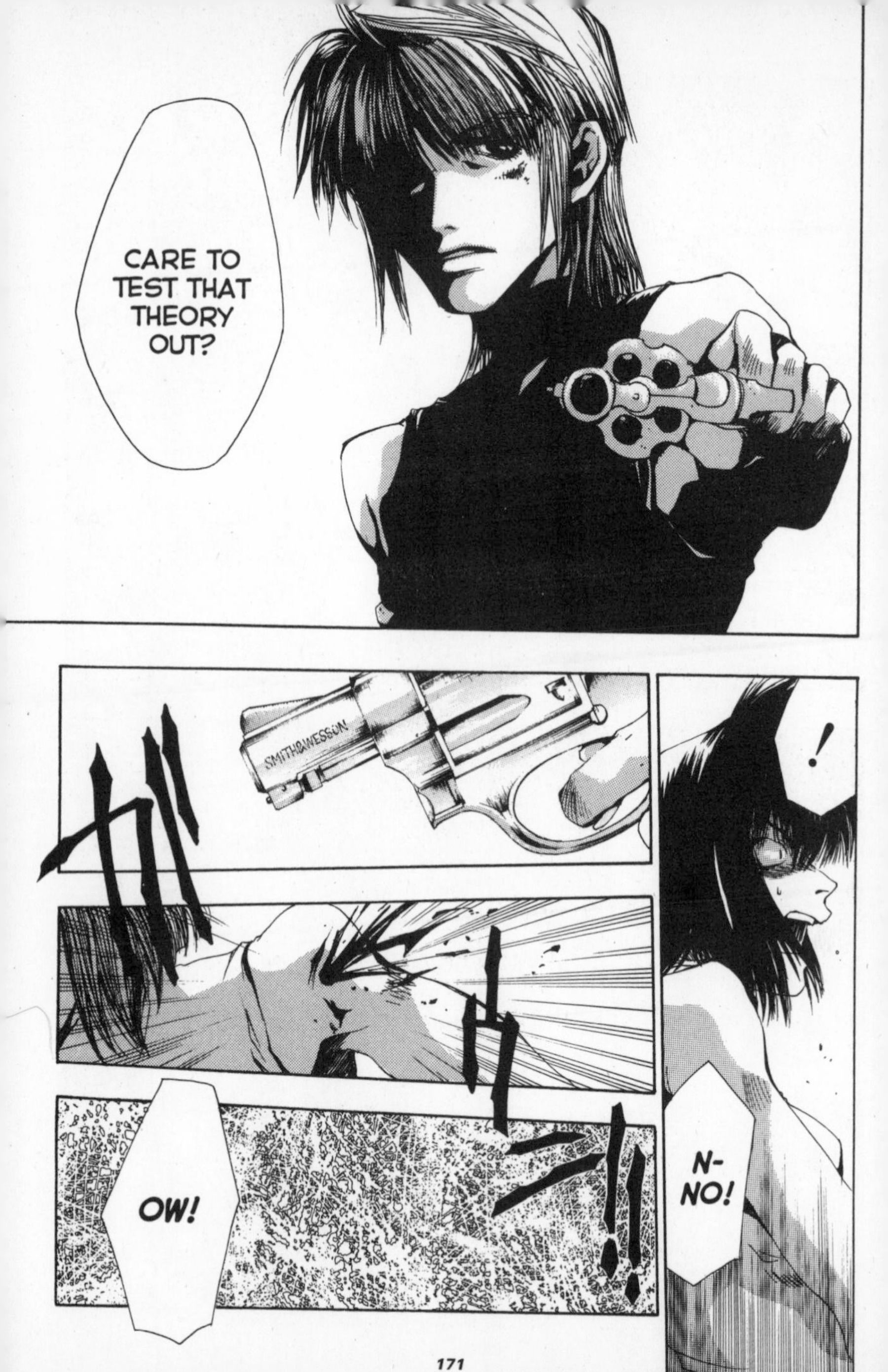

CARE TO TEST THAT THEORY OUT?

SMITH&WESSON

!

N-NO!

OW!

LOOK AT THAT.
AAAAAAGH!
I GUESS IMMORTALS CAN FEEL PAIN LIKE THE REST OF US.
IF I HIT YOUR HEAD OR HEART...
...I BET IT'D HURT LIKE HELL.
NO!
PLEASE, DON'T!

THIS IS STUPID.
YAAAAAAH!
AAAAH!
THIS IS REALLY STUPID.
GYAAAAAH!

SHIT, MAN! TORTURE?

THIS ISN'T LIKE YOU!

NOT LIKE ME...?

THEN WHAT *IS* LIKE ME?

WHAT'S THAT SUPPOSED TO...

THAT HURT!

WHAT THE HELL ARE YOU DOING?!

HIT ME.

HOW VERY SUDDEN.
THAT CRUELTY IN SANZO JUST VANISHED COMPLETELY.
I SUPPOSE IT COULDN'T STAND UP TO GOKU.
YOU.
ANSWER ME SOMETHING.

THE OLD ONE'S S- SOMEWHERE AROUND THE CASTLE.
YOURS IS IN THE CHEST.
THE ONE RIGHT BEHIND YOU.
THERE?
はっ
SANZO, WATCH IT!

GAHAH!

SANZO!
ARE YOU OKAY?!
HAKKAI, FIX HIM!
CALM DOWN, GOK--
?!
WHAT?

HEH HEH. DO YOU L-LIKE MY SCORPION CLAWS?
THE POISON IN THEM'S FATAL.
YOU... YOU STUPID CREEP!

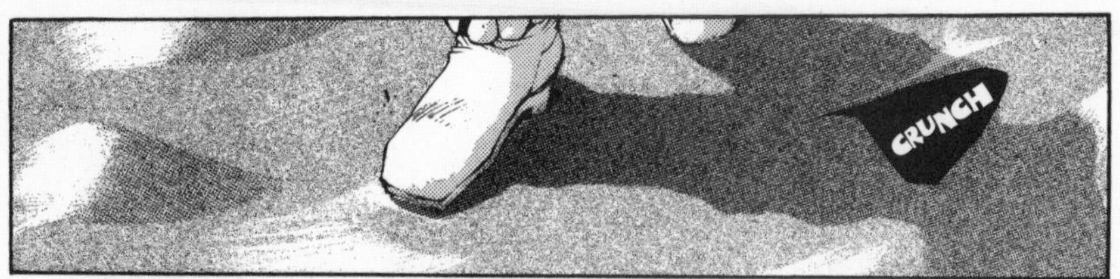

DAMN. HOT ENOUGH FOR YA?

MM.

BUT THAT'S STRANGE.

ACCORDING TO THE REPORT, THE CASTLE SHOULD BE HERE.

——?

SOMETHING WRONG, DOKUGAKU?
UH, NO.
THERE'S JUST SOME WHITE THING BURIED OVER THERE.
ザッ
?!
HEY, LOOK AT THAT!
ISN'T THAT THE, UH...
オォ
オ...

IT SURE LOOKS LIKE SANZO'S JEEP.
?
WHAT'S IT DOING HERE?
CHEEEP
CHEEP
CHEEEP
I DON'T BELIEVE THIS.
SANZO AND THE OTHERS ARE HERE!

オリジナルビデオアニメ よこくへん

OVA予告編

HELLO, SANZO AND COMPANY!
THE NEXT "ACCIDENT" IS ABOUT TO BEGIN.
I DO HOPE EVERYONE'S READY.

PASSING THROUGH THA VILLAGE...
永安酒家
...I TAKE IT YOU MADE SOME NEW FRIENDS?
YOUR JEEP IS *AMAZING!* YOU'RE ALL VERY WELCOME HERE. ♡
AND YOU'RE WELCOME OVER *HERE*, SWEETHEART. ♡
Sha Gojyo (Voice Actor: Kouichi Yamadera)
THESE'RE FIREWORKS?
Son Goku (Voice Actor: Kosuke Okano)
THERE'S A FESTIVAL TODAY.
COME CELEBRATE WITH US!

AH, FICKLE LIFE.

ACCIDENTS ARE SUCH A SHAME.

SOUNDS LIKE SOME KINDA FIRECRACK--
HYA HA HA!
HA HA!

!!!
HYA HA HA HA HA HA!
......
THAT'S NOT FRICKIN' F-FUNNY.

ENSUI CONSIDERS HIMSELF AN EXPLOSION ARTIST.
BUT PLEASE.
I CAN'T JUST IGNORE THIS!
HE'S REALLY MORE OF A MAD SCIENTIST THAN ANYTHING.
YAONE...
MM.
COME, KOUGAIJI DEAR. DON'T BE SHY.
CALL ME MOMMY.

ISN'T IT BEAUTI-FUL?
THE MOMENT A SOUL SHATTERS IS TRULY *ART!*
GET AWAY FROM HIM, JEEP!
DON'T WORRY-- I'LL LET HIM GO.
YOU'RE MY FRIENDS.
BROTHERS, EVEN.
FELLOW YOUKAI.

THE COUNT-DOWN BEGINS.
パチッ
WHAT'S THAT NOISE?
IT CAN'T BE...!
THAT'S RIGHT, BOYS.
YOUR PET IS NOW CARRYING A TIME BOMB.
I CAN'T GET IT OUT.
IT'S EATEN INTO JEEP'S NERVES!

05:45
YOU HAVE *SIX HOURS.*
WELL...
FIVE AND THREE-QUARTERS, REALLY.
LEAVE US ALONE, YA STUPID PSYCHO!
WHAT'D WE EVER DO TO YOU?!
THESE ARE ONLY ACCIDENTS.
AND ACCIDENTS ARE *NOBODY'S* FAULT.
......
PRE-PARE TO DIE.

オリジナル ビデオ　アニメ　アンド　ディー　ブイ　ディー　さいゆうき

OVA&DVD最遊記

OVA & DVD *SAIYUKI*

...AH, SCREW IT.

WE GIVE UP.

WE'VE MADE OUR DECISION.

NOW IS THE TIME WE DIE. ♡

A NEW BREED OF TACTIC...HOPEFULLY.

I ALREADY TOLD YOU-- NOTHING IS REAL.

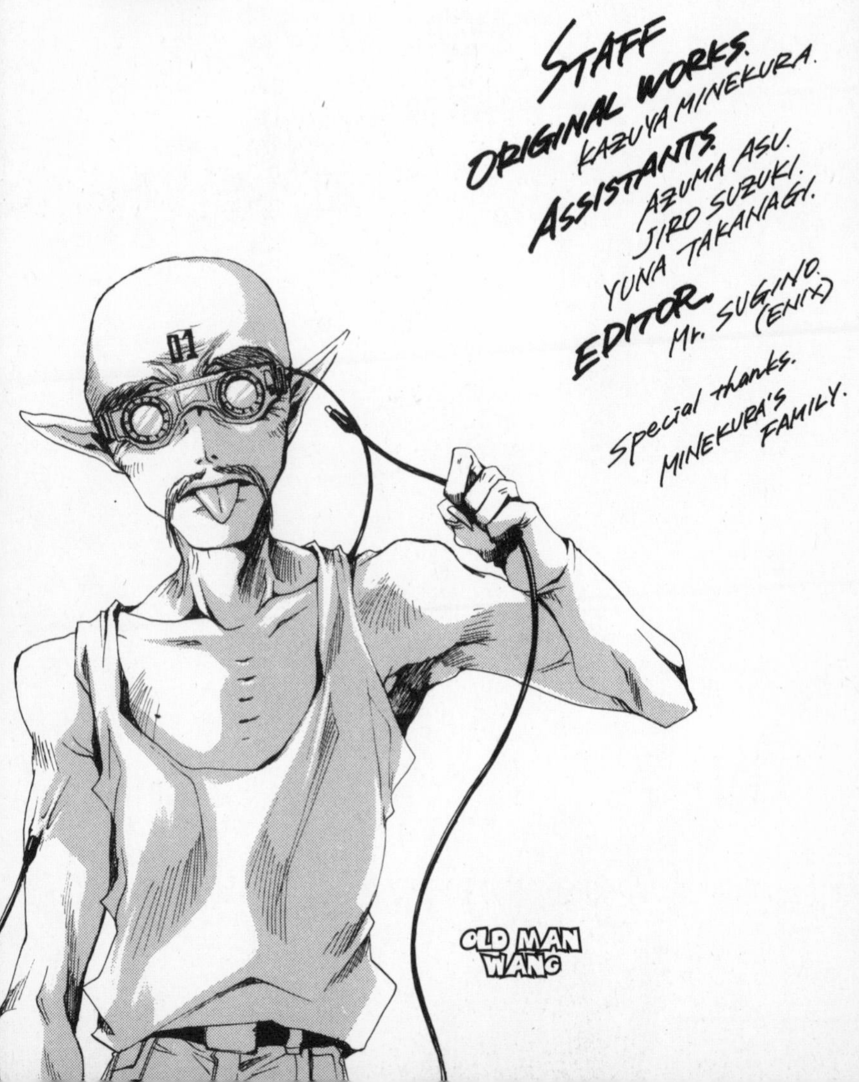

GETTING WET IS STUPID IN THIS COLD.
to the skin,
KAZUYA MINEKURA 1999.

Get soaked

SOUND EFFECT CHART

THE FOLLOWING IS A LIST OF THE SOUND EFFECTS USED IN SAIYUKI. EACH SOUND IS LABELED BY PAGE AND PANEL NUMBER, SEPARATED BY A PERIOD. THE FIRST DESCRIPTION (IN BOLD) IS THE PHONETIC READING OF THE JAPANESE, AND IS FOLLOWED BY THE EQUIVALENT ENGLISH SOUND OR A DESCRIPTION.

GIRI!

THIS USEFUL SOUND EFFECT HAS A COUPLE OF FUNCTIONS: IT CAN BE EITHER THE SOUND OF GRINDING TEETH OR TWO COMBATANTS STRUGGLING AGAINST EACH OTHER.

9.2 GOHOH: GLUB
13.4 GATA: CLATTER
13.7 ZAA: (FALLING RAIN)
15.2 ZAA: (FALLING RAIN)
15.3 GUH: NUDGE
16.3 ZAA (FALLING RAIN)
18.2 ZUKI: THROB
18.3 PUHAA: PUFF
21.1 DORO: MUDDY
21.3 PAN!: FWAP!
22.2 BOSO BOSO: WHISPER
22.5 BIKU: SURPRISE
22.6 ZAH: STEP
26.5 UGAA: GRR
27.4 SU: (MOVING SILENTLY)
30.7 ZAWA ZAWA: CHATTER
32.2 GATAN: CLATTER
33.2 KII: CREAK
33.4 BASA: FLUTTER
37.4 GATA: CLATTER
37.5 GACHA: LATCH
38.4 KII: CREAK
38.5 PATAN: SHUT
43.3 ZAH: DODGE
43.4 PASHI: GRAB
44.1 DOGOH: SLAM
44.2 GAKU: DROOP
44.3 KEBA GOHO: COUGH

DOKUN!

IN MOST MANGA, A PLEASANT LITTLE "DOKI DOKI" IS THE PREFERRED SOUND FOR HEARTBEATS, BUT IN SAIYUKI, THEY NEEDED TO KICK IT UP A NOTCH. "DOKUN" IS THE SOUND OF A PARTICULARLY STRONG HEARTBEAT, USUALLY RESERVED FOR MOMENTS OF EXTREME SHOCK OR DEMONIC TRANSFORMATION.

44.4 GAH: GRAB
45.1 BAKU: PUNCH
45.2 ZAZAH: WHOOSH
45.3 GUH: WIPE
46.5 GAUN: BANG
46.6 HIKU: TWITCH
47.1 GACHA: LATCH
47.3 BAH: MOVE
47.4 HYU: WHOOSH
47.5 PASHI: KICK
47.6 KASHA: CLUNK
48.1 GO: LIFT...
48.2 ZUSHA: SLAM
48.3 GIRI: GRIT
49.3 DAH: DASH
49.5 TAAN: THUD
50.3 ZAH: RUSH
50.4 GAH: KICK
50.6 BAH: SHOVE
51.1 JAH...: THUD
51.4 KURU: TURN
51.4 WAKU WAKU: GIDDY
52.1 GOPAA: WHACK
52-53 DOSA: THUD
53.3 DAH: DASH
53.4 ZAH: GRAB
53.5 BAH: MOVE
53.5 KICHU: SCREACH

NIKO!

(OR JUST NI)

IT TAKES 26 MUSCLES TO SMILE, OR JUST TWO KATAKANA! "NIKO," REPEATED AS MUCH AS YOU WANT FOR EMPHASIS, GIVES THE READER AN INDICATION OF JUST HOW BIG A SMILE IS.

56.1 ZAKU...: WHOOSH
56.2 KOPOPO: GLUB GLUB
56.5 ZU: SLURP
56.6 ZUZUZU: SLURP SLURP SLURP
59.3 GOTSUN GOTSUN: NOD NOD
60.1 UHAA: WOO-HOO!
60.2 GYAA GYAA: RANT RANT
60.3 GUGIGI: SQUEEZE (HEADLOCK)
64.1 GATA: CLATTER
65.2 ZURU...: SLIDE
65.6 GOSO: RUSTLE
66.1 JARA...: CRACK
66.5 GOH: WHOOSH
67.1 DOGOH!: SLAM
67.2 DOSA: THUD
67.3 JARI: SCRAPE
68.2 DOKUN: THADUMP
70.1 GIRI: SCUFF
70.3 KOTOH: CLULNK
74.4 JII: STARE

SHIN!

THE SOUND OF SILENCE. THE PERFECT "SOUND" EFFECT TO PUNCTUATE THOSE UNCOMFORTABLE MOMENTS WHERE THE LACK OF ANY ACTUAL SOUNDS JUST ISN'T SUFFICIENT. FOR EMPHASIS, YOU'LL USUALLY SEE A LONG LINE IN BETWEEN THE "SHI" AND THE "N," INDICATING PROLONGED SILENCE.

112.1 TOH: GLOMP
113.2 KATAH: CLUNK
115.1 GABAH: GLOMP
115.3 BAN: SLAM
116.2 BAH: RUSH

HAH!

THIS IS ONE OF THE MOST COMMON SOUNDS YOU'LL SEE IN MANGA. IT'S USED TO INDICATE SURPRISE AND IS USUALLY EQUIVALENT TO "GASP!" "H" ISN'T NECESSARILY VOCALIZED, THOUGH.

121.2: KAH: FLASH
122.1-4 DODODODO: RUUUUMBLE
122.4 CHAKI: CLICK
123.1 BURORORO: VROOM
123.3 DODODO: RUUUMBLE
124.1 DODO: RUUUMBLE
124.2 DODODO: RUUUMBLE
126.2 BASA: RUSTLE
127.3 SHIIIN: SILENCE
131.5 ZAAH: WHOOSH
133.2 OOOH: HOWLING WIND
133.3 KA KA KA: CLICK
138.5 PETAPETA: WAVE WAVE
139.2 ZUN ZUN: SNIFF SNIFF
139.5 PAAA: YAAAY
141.2 OOO: HOLWING WIND
142.4 ZAAA: HOWLING WIND
143.1 ZUBU: SINK
143.2 GAKUN: DROOP
143.3 ZUZUZU: SINK SINK SINK
143.4 GAKUN: DROOP

76.4 PIKU: PERK
77.2-3 ZAAH: WHOOSH
79.1 GUH: GRAB
79.3 BUSHU: SCOOP OUT
79.4 PASHI: SPIT
79.5 BISHA: SPLAT
81.2 SOH: SHIVER
81.3 GUH: GRAB
81.4 ZAZA: RUN RUN
82.1 BAH: GLOMP
82.2 DOSA: THUD
82.3 KYOTO: LOOK
86.2 GATAKU: SHIVER
86.3 DAH: DASH
86.4 GOH: WHOOSH
87.2 PAAN: BANG
90-91 OOOH: HOWLING WIND
91.3 SHARI: SCUFF
92.2 OOO: HOWLING WIND
93.4 BAH: SIT

ZAA!

YOU'LL SEE THIS ONE A LOT IN *SAIYUKI*. "ZAA" INDICATES A DRAMATIC APPEARANCE. IF YOU WANT TO MAKE A LASTING IMPRESSION, ALWAYS COME IN WITH A COOL POSE AND A BIG "ZAA!"

96.2 OOOH: HOWLING WIND
98.2 GOUN: BOOM
101.2 GAH: GRAB
108.3 TAH: TMP
111.4 GYAA GYAA: RANT RANT

143.4 GAKUN: DROOP
144.1 ZUZUZU: SINK SINK SINK
144.2 GAH: GRAB
145.1 ZUZUZU: SINK SINK SINK
145.3 ZUBA: SINK
145.4 ZUZUZU: SINK SINK SINK
146.2 ZUZUZU: SINK SINK SINK
146.3 GIRI GIRI: GRIT
146.4 ZUZU: SINK SINK
147.1 BAH: SHOVE

ZAWA!

NO ONE REALLY CARES WHAT ALL THOSE EXTRAS IN THE BACKGROUND ARE SAYING, RIGHT? THAT'S WHY MANGA-KA USE THIS HANDY SOUND EFFECT TO INDICATE BACKGROUND CHATTER. YOU'LL SEE IT HOVERING OVER CROWDED CITY STREETS OR CLASSROOMS THROUGHOUT MANGA. IT CAN ALSO BE USED TO INDICATE THE SOUND OF WIND BLOWING THROUGH THE LEAVES OF A TREE. AIN'T THAT SWEET?

147.2 ZUZU: SINK SINK
147.3 ZU...: SINK...
147.4 ZAA: RUSTLE
148.2 OOO: HOWLING WIND
150.2 HOH: GASP
153.3 FU...: SIGH
154.1 PIKU: TWITCH
154.3 PATA: THUD
154.6 KAH: CLACK
155.5 GISHI: CREAK
158.2 PIKU: TWITCH
158.4 PAAN: SLAP
159.4 GAN GAN: CLANG CLANG
160.1 GASHA GASHA: CLANG CLANG
160.5 ZU: SLIP
161.1 ZURUZURU: SLIP
162.2 BOTO: PLOP
163.2 ZAKU: SKITTER
166.3 BAKII: PUNK/WHACK
167.1 GUI: TUG
167.5 HYU: WHOOSH
168.1 BAKI: PUNCH/WHACK
168.2 DOSA: THUD
169.2 ZAH: STEP
171.4 GAUN: BANG
173.1 GAUN: BANG
173.2 GAUN: BANG
173.3 GAUN: BANG
174.1 BAN: SLAM
174.3 GUI: GRAB
175.4 GAN: KICK
177.5 ZEH ZEH: PANT PANT
178.4 HA: GASP
178.5 SHAKII: GLEAM
179.1 BUSHU: THUNK
182.1 OOOH: HOWLING WIND
183.1 ZAH: STEP
184.4 OOOH: HOWLING WIND
188.3 WAAA: LOUD CROWD
189.1 BURORORO: VROOM
190.1 GOH: WHOOSH
190.2 DOOON: BOOOM
190.3 GOOOO: HOWLING WIND
191.2 DAH: DASH
193.2 BAH: RUSH
194.1 PACHIN: SNAP

SANTA INOUE
TOKYO TRIBES
Turnin' up tha heat on tha streets of Tokyo!
TOKYOPOP
EXPLICIT CONTENT
PARENTAL ADVISORY
EXPLICIT CONTENT
OT
OLDER TEEN AGE 16+
©1998 SANTASTIC! ©2004 TOKYOPOP Inc. All rights reserved
www.TOKYOPOP.com

TOKYOPOP®

GETBACKERS™

They get back what shouldn't be gone... most of the time.

EXPLICIT CONTENT
PARENTAL ADVISORY
EXPLICIT CONTENT

OT
OLDER TEEN
AGE 16+

ALSO AVAILABLE FROM TOKYOPOP®

MANGA

.HACK//LEGEND OF THE TWILIGHT
@LARGE
ABENOBASHI: MAGICAL SHOPPING ARCADE
A.I. LOVE YOU
AI YORI AOSHI
ANGELIC LAYER
ARM OF KANNON
BABY BIRTH
BATTLE ROYALE
BATTLE VIXENS
BRAIN POWERED
BRIGADOON
B'TX
CANDIDATE FOR GODDESS, THE
CARDCAPTOR SAKURA
CARDCAPTOR SAKURA - MASTER OF THE CLOW
CHOBITS
CHRONICLES OF THE CURSED SWORD
CLAMP SCHOOL DETECTIVES
CLOVER
COMIC PARTY
CONFIDENTIAL CONFESSIONS
CORRECTOR YUI
COWBOY BEBOP
COWBOY BEBOP: SHOOTING STAR
CRAZY LOVE STORY
CRESCENT MOON
CROSS
CULDCEPT
CYBORG 009
D•N•ANGEL
DEMON DIARY
DEMON ORORON, THE
DEUS VITAE
DIABOLO
DIGIMON
DIGIMON TAMERS
DIGIMON ZERO TWO
DOLL
DRAGON HUNTER
DRAGON KNIGHTS
DRAGON VOICE
DREAM SAGA
DUKLYON: CLAMP SCHOOL DEFENDERS
EERIE QUEERIE!
ERICA SAKURAZAWA: COLLECTED WORKS
ET CETERA
ETERNITY
EVIL'S RETURN
FAERIES' LANDING
FAKE
FLCL
FLOWER OF THE DEEP SLEEP
FORBIDDEN DANCE
FRUITS BASKET
G GUNDAM
GATEKEEPERS
GETBACKERS
GIRL GOT GAME
GIRLS EDUCATIONAL CHARTER
GRAVITATION
GTO
GUNDAM BLUE DESTINY
GUNDAM SEED ASTRAY
GUNDAM WING
GUNDAM WING: BATTLEFIELD OF PACIFISTS
GUNDAM WING: ENDLESS WALTZ
GUNDAM WING: THE LAST OUTPOST (G-UNIT)
GUYS' GUIDE TO GIRLS
HANDS OFF!
HAPPY MANIA
HARLEM BEAT
HYPER RUNE
I.N.V.U.
IMMORTAL RAIN
INITIAL D
INSTANT TEEN: JUST ADD NUTS
ISLAND
JING: KING OF BANDITS
JING: KING OF BANDITS - TWILIGHT TALES
JULINE
KARE KANO
KILL ME, KISS ME
KINDAICHI CASE FILES, THE
KING OF HELL
KODOCHA: SANA'S STAGE
LAMENT OF THE LAMB
LEGAL DRUG
LEGEND OF CHUN HYANG, THE
LES BIJOUX
LOVE HINA
LUPIN III
LUPIN III: WORLD'S MOST WANTED
MAGIC KNIGHT RAYEARTH I
MAGIC KNIGHT RAYEARTH II
MAHOROMATIC: AUTOMATIC MAIDEN
MAN OF MANY FACES
MARMALADE BOY
MARS
MARS: HORSE WITH NO NAME
MINK
MIRACLE GIRLS
MIYUKI-CHAN IN WONDERLAND
MODEL
MOURYOU KIDEN
MY LOVE
NECK AND NECK
ONE
ONE I LOVE, THE
PARADISE KISS
PARASYTE
PASSION FRUIT
PEACH GIRL
PEACH GIRL: CHANGE OF HEART

STOP!

This is the back of the book. You wouldn't want to spoil a great ending!

This book is printed "manga-style," in the authentic Japanese right-to-left format. Since none of the artwork has been flipped or altered, readers get to experience the story just as the creator intended. You've been asking for it, so TOKYOPOP® delivered: authentic, hot-off-the-press, and far more fun!

DIRECTIONS

If this is your first time reading manga-style, here's a quick guide to help you understand how it works.

It's easy... just start in the top right panel and follow the numbers. Have fun, and look for more 100% authentic manga from TOKYOPOP®!